ink
for
two

by abbie amy

art by sidney jean

For Sidney

who turned
my words
into art

A friend who reminds me
that I have a gift
A friend who also
gets drunk with me over text

Sidney Jean
sigh sign sing

You make my cheeks ache
You let me cry
when my spirit breaks

Thank you
for your art

Thank you more
for your generous
heart

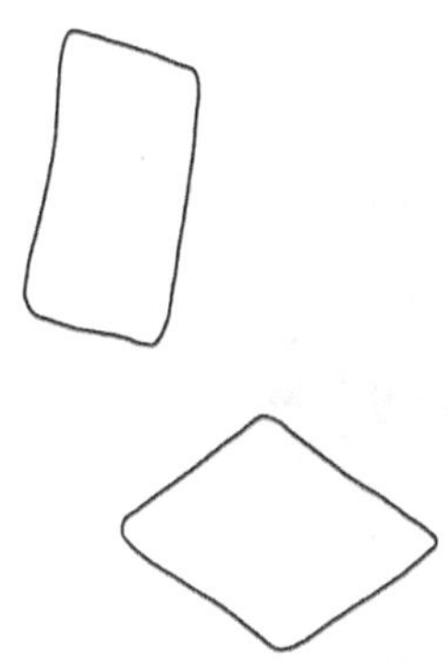

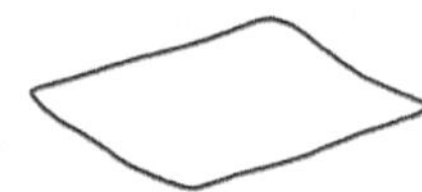

They come in threes
my mother says

Inside there lives a monster
in the cellar of her heart
He bides there always waiting
residing in the dark

She feels him stir within her
against her flesh and bone
He has woken from his slumber
and threatens to impose

He creeps inside her organs
and turns her blood to wine
He drinks until her body falls
broken from inside

I bathe in the silence of the night
and reach out and touch it
I hold each whisper of
darkness in my hand
Stillness is tangible

I swallow the moon
only to drown in the stars
There are too many of them
for me to know

I am not afraid of the night
I am afraid of never understanding
what it can do

I open my arms wide
and invite the late hour in
We embrace each other
as though we're old friends

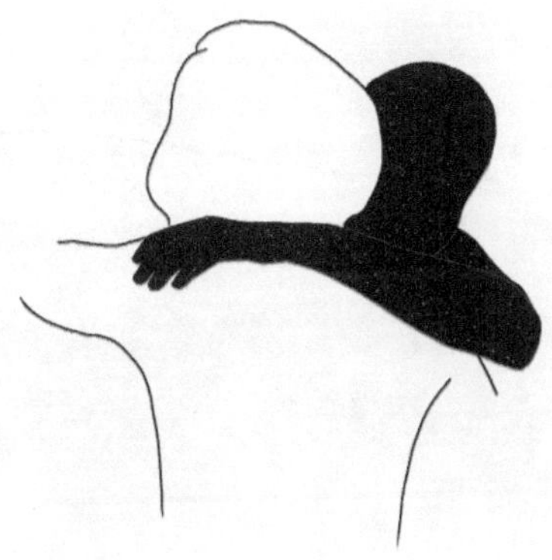

Our lives are a constant coin toss
A balance between right and wrong
Sometimes the coin lands on neither
and we ponder this all day long

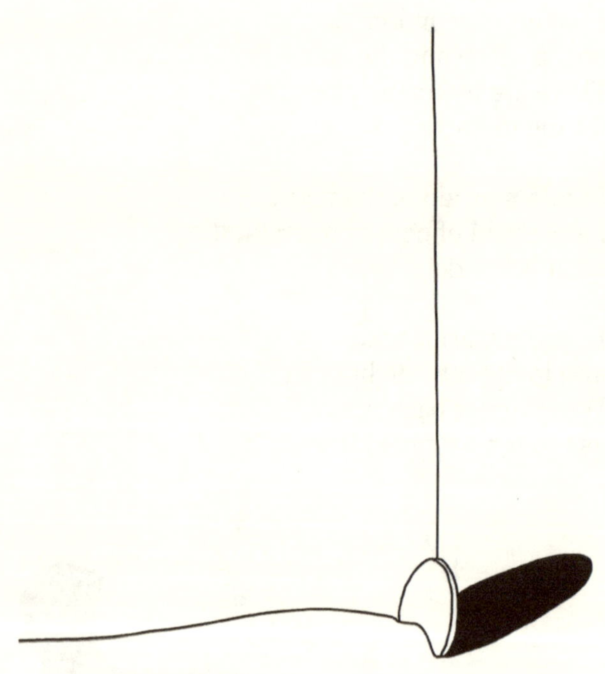

The bear has her claws out
She's fighting your battle again
You can play the mouse
as much as you please
we all know you're
the serpent underneath
You can slither around the truth
lure others with your falsehoods
and allow lies to pour out
like running water
a river to drown us all
I know you love that boy
You would choke him to death
with your affection
But his heart is tied to the jungle
to the sweet girl
who blossoms under him
What are you going to do?
Get the bear to confess
what you cannot?
You pin your heartaches onto me
until I start to rot

I don't have enough
there's just too much
I would kill for more
can we keep this short
I'm an open door
I'm the ocean floor
I am the time that you need

I am the time that can't be

The curtain starts to open
the scene begins to play
Something precious stolen
that second week of May

The people watch her pass
cautious as she goes
She cannot stand their whispers
at what they think they know

A body on the carpet
a body with no orbit
Her world now plagued with agony
to the monster she will forfeit

I am on the precipice of something
too high to see it clearly
too scared to ever be ready
No one has a net
No one stands below
I'm not quite willing
for someone to really know

But
there's a desire in their eyes
I watch it light and die
as their grubby fingers reach inside
where there's nothing left to find

Faces arranged in horror
and I tell them
it's okay
I'm the one who's empty
watching love that likes to leave me
You won't ever be this way

We hardly touched
and yet on my shoulders
are fingerprints of potential love

I sit awkwardly
in the lap of luxury
there's icing sugar
on my black leggings

My hair flicks up
I think it's too short
They call me
by my sister's name
I'm too polite to complain

Your phone is broken
You call me anyway
Seated at the piano
hands I am yet to know

There's an echoing sadness
in both of us
but hopefulness
is the song
you decide to play

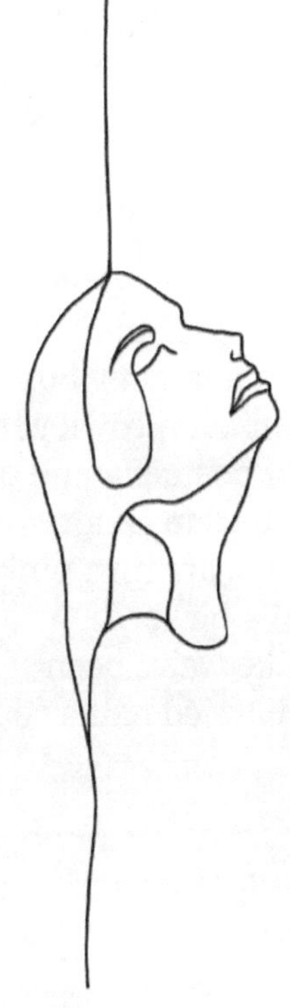

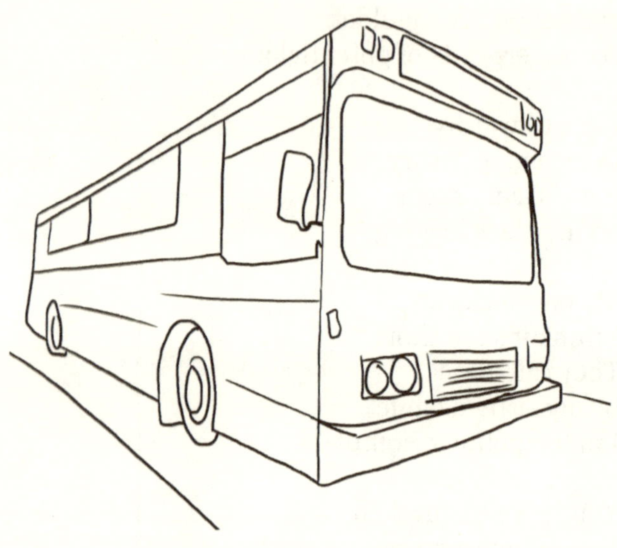

He reads to me
about feminism
on a moving bus
An overgrown garden
of nostalgia and opinions
The sun is hot
my ears turn pink
We bicker
like we've been
married half a century

Cherry-stained cheeks
A look-alike friend
The summer heat bleeds
A three-piece bends
Stolen grapes in the park
Greeting jealousy
An infectious laugh
Dancing freely
A drunken promise
The joke's on you
Killed it
Saw it
It should have been you

Your words catch
in your throat
Your eyes speak it anyway
Goodbye on a street
I think we did okay
Now a red dress is waiting
I write this down
the next day

Keep them
closed
then you
can't see
the people
who you love
the people
who will leave

Her heart recoils with fear
knowing what is to come
The monster will return here
the damage will be done

She searches for her father
the man who was her saviour
She cries and pleads
then listens
the grave gives no answer

The monster's name means grief
he lives within us all
Just waiting for the moment
to have us in his thrall

Do not give
your thoughts
and prayers
Give me your
spare kidney
and the bones
inside your fingers
and then all the
useless brutal pain
that insists and lingers

—Sympathy

Under the covers
I want to hide
and bury myself
beneath
a hundred layers
of gossamer
to trick me
into sleep

The dandelion knows me
that flower is my friend
I've loved her since childhood
she carries my
innocence in her seeds
I wish upon her
when plucked from the ground
I ask for success and love
Yet when my breath
blows out her life
I am suddenly much older
the dandelion
I'm now unworthy of

My friend tells me
that once we walk
through the gate
I have to let all the words
I cannot say escape
It's not that easy
but he's here
and I'm here
and he's saying
that this is what
he wants to hear
So I tell him
I try to contain
a human life in words

—A Waxing Moon

I go to his study
I open up his diary
I see the weeks ahead
The plans laid out
by the hand of the dead
Man proposes
God disposes

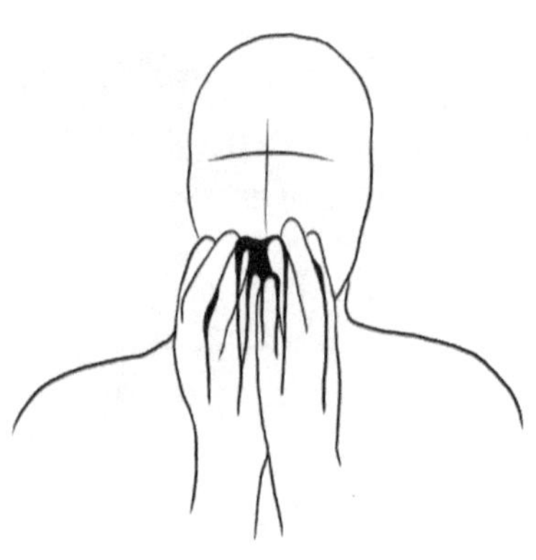

I breathe like a whisper
but run sentences
together in chaos
My laugh rouses
birds from nests
My spirit cuts
the sky in two
I could crack open
a frozen lake
by the visceral nature
of my dreams alone
I am the colour of
pale lavender
perfumed with intuition
but plagued with wasps
and not honey bees
A new layer of skin
might fix me
the chance to start afresh
Or perhaps I will have to wait
until the bright dawn of possibility
comes around too late

A letter sealed
with yearning
My lips pressed
to paper

Collect your mail
in the afternoon
and use my words
to escape her

A prayer a day
keeps the guilt away

She leaves a basket of flowers
upon my doorstep
The tulips say
I'm sorry
I'd like to sit with you
at lunch on Monday

How do I tell her
that I just buried my father
That I don't care
whose shoulders I brush
while pretending to eat my lunch
There was a coffin
containing someone
Someone who used to
swing me in his arms
when I ran to him
A little girl with excited eyes
in her father's arms
she could fly

I ignore the flowers
On Monday I eat alone

And God said
You are mine
before he
claimed
another
for his own

She is the wildflower
who desires a love
to feed her rain and sun
and create the
swing of the season
She can grow on her own
but how special would it be
to have someone
nurturing her into a garden
for all the world to see

We see our insecurities
perfected on the faces
of strangers

I wish my brain and body could have a talk
I hate how they refuse to get along
My brain has locked that door
sold the key for a price she thinks
will help her more

The body is the enemy
Any other narrative
will be treated warily

But I'm working!
my body longs to say in celebration
I can hold you up
I endure
My lungs expand without rest
My heart refuses to stop
I am alive
and would like to get to know you

She receives no reply
The brain is too lost in herself
to hear the quiet lament

Youth is not a mirror
it is not a fountain nor a truth
It is the wind in your hair
the laughter that crumples bellies
the chaos of loving
the turn of the day
Youth is the feeling inside you
despite what the flesh will say

It was the people around me
with stares that look not see
With promises of holidays
before a sudden desire to leave
This is why abandonment
comes free with every attachment
I have accepted that I am Medusa
my face an unwanted odyssey
The longing in my eyes
turns the rejection to stone
for everyone to throw at me

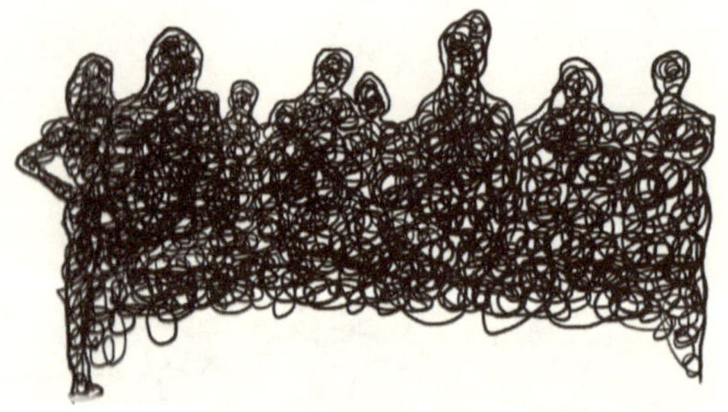

Induced on a Wednesday
tempted into the world
by falling dreams
Arms to hold me
until I could hold myself
Living with a wealth
that even as a child
I knew wouldn't last
Proven right
by the freshly staged sight
blue and grey on a human face
All the love I had
taken away

There's a ladder
leading to the attic
I used to hold it steady
My body at the ready
I was terrified my dad
might fall

It wasn't a ladder in the end
A red desk chair
A forgotten cup of tea
A page in a book he was reading
No final performance from me

The bottles promise life
The doctors say
Just exercise!
But here I am a daughter
still holding on to a ladder
no longer bearing her father

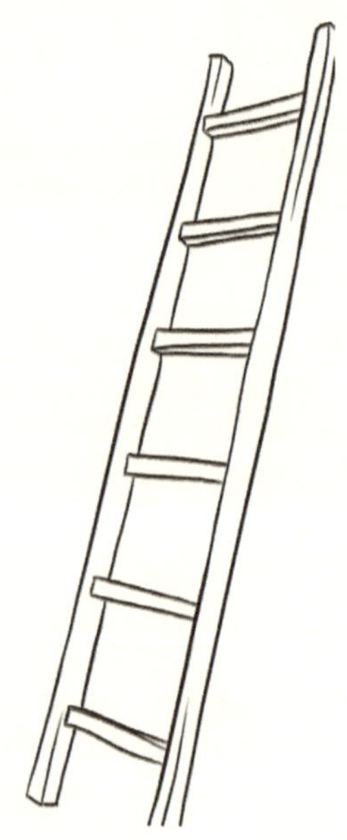

We have a jigsaw of memories
I was putting on blush
from a compact filled
with the colour of rose
I threw it out after
I must have been wearing
my school jumper
Picasso would have made art
from the scene waiting for me
Weeping Woman
this is not for my eyes
What century have I fallen in
for parents do not cry
The phone
I needed the cordless phone
Downstairs
Screaming at the operator
She instructed and I instructed
How did I end the call?
I vaguely remember
paramedics entering the hall
Sitting on the kitchen floor
The world laughed
and the resounding chant

He's gone
He's gone
He's gone

When someone dies
do not send flowers
Last time
they were spilling out of the living room
in hues of magenta and gold
and I wasn't sold
on how they were meant
to make anything better
We were watering for weeks
the petals shrinking and browning
fluttering to the ground
it whispered of time passing
Do not send a metaphor for life
to those who mourn

When the school bell goes
I trundle home to a family who is trying
Yet I sit alone
surrounded by tulips and fragrant lilies
Surrounded by nothing
I miss the only person
who could comfort me
I sit in a makeshift greenhouse
as a flower takes one last breath—

and falls

She snores softly and wakes gently
unless she dreams of death
She never explained
when you took her in
Two arms
Two types of love
Her hands are bound in loss

You're okay
in the tune
of a plea
Please, Abbie
it's me

Abbie?

But some hearts
are too
grotesque
to see

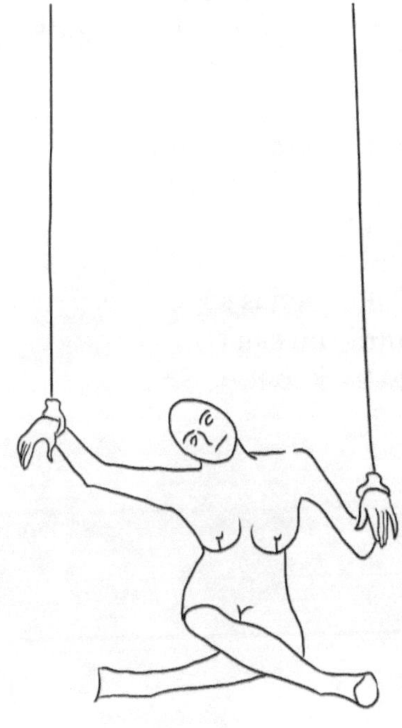

What is untouched
until it is plundered?
There is new comprehension
that you are no longer
one of the children
You cannot sit at the dining table
and join in the conversation
They shoot you using a gun
loaded with apprehension
You have seen
more at seventeen
than the teacher
sitting in front of you
reading your essays
picking apart your thoughts
with red crosses
as though she knows
how to grade your losses
Death took away
a parent
and an innocence
Childhood is so tedious
until you can't
go back to it

abbie amy

There is a sadness in me
I'm too scared to touch
I don't know if it will shatter
or if I will combust

He was born on the cusp of war
to a mother who would raise him
and a father who wouldn't know him
until the bleeding of men
came to the inevitable end

When I think about my father
and his childhood
I see this
A small kitchen
A woman with an apron
A cobbled street
A wired bicycle racing around the bend
Inhale and exhale the wind

My father became his father
The role of provider
There were three before
who had shut the door
We leave them at
the back of the draw
The father of two daughters
The husband of the best of wives
The twinkle in his eye

Half a decade
I'm trying not to forget
This is about my father
This is all I have left

The calendar is on fire
There's the crisp
lull of autumn
Waves of pastel
splash upon the dawn
Put on your veil
he's hidden
under velvet
You left it too long
You try to make up
with other people
what was
and
now
is gone

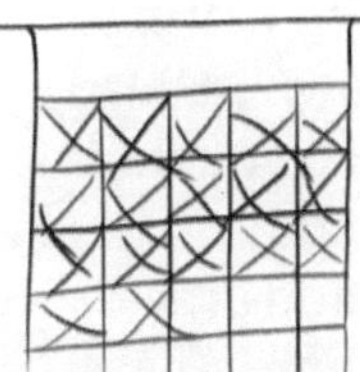

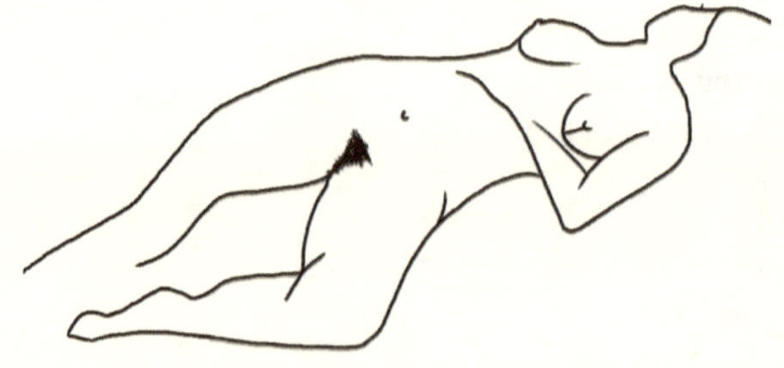

I'll never admit
this out loud
so I'm writing
it down instead
When you find
my body
old and grey
tell him
what I should
have said

I feel you in the back
corner of my heart
You're a myth they tell
when the sky goes dark

There's a friendship
might be more
I let myself ponder
what's behind that door

I take every insecurity
let it manifest that summer evening
Then write it out
in blue boxes
imagining your possible responses

Could you touch me
Might you love me
I break shoulders easily
My own bones snap quite frequently

I bite my nails
The whoosh of *sent*
into the questioning vortex

Dots then your reply

I'm driving over now
Wait for me outside

Beginnings
are brilliant
curiosities
They are
the wonder
of the unknown
the static
of what could be
An endless dawn
of possible
possibilities

The night after is always the hardest
It's the hour when I'm the closest
I can see your face clearly
not just a vague outline
but a definite linear shape
I can trace it from memory
I can feel the warmth of your shoulder
where I brush you in good humour
Tactile
Close
Companion
Not mine
I can hear the bray of your heart
the candour of your laugh
the way you trip over sentences
trying to explain what you shouldn't
I tell myself to go to bed
How can I?
When in the morning
the rising sun will overcome
the clarity of tonight

I want to make up stories
and live in them with you

We're under the
influence
of the late hour

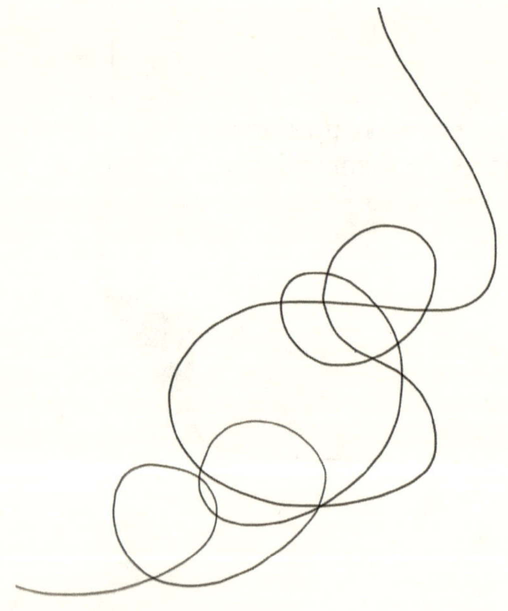

There's a boy in my bed
Have I lost my head
He swears we're just friends
but I feel his body bend
and I know his words are lies

Soft limbs
Soft heart
Hard bones
Cold mark

We sleep intertwined
praying that the morning
might just forget to rise

I can see why people have affairs
It's easy to get lost in something
that doesn't quite belong to you

You cover me in bandages
swaddled in the promise of safety
I haven't been feeling myself lately
That can happen after the moon
pulls the tide and you watch
the ocean leave itself out to dry
You smooth ointment along my arms
press lavender to my throat
It will help you sleep
is the assurance
After thanks I ask for guidance
I'd like to know how to do it myself
You hush me against the pillows
pull the blanket close
I'm asleep with reassurance
Why would I need help
from anyone else

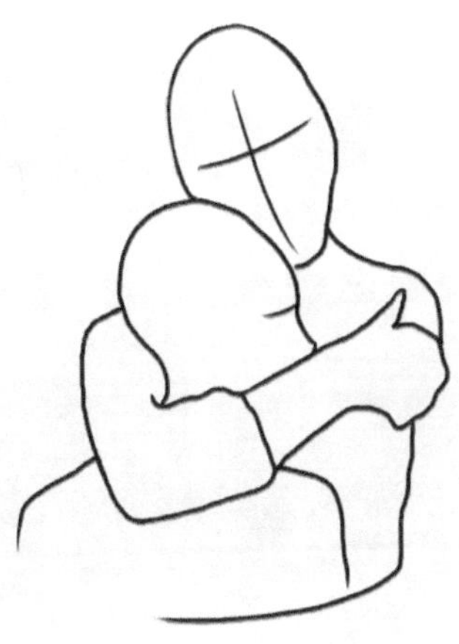

I write around his heart
for fear that if I get too close
it will all just fall apart
I've watched it fail before
people once saturated
now black and white
on the carpeted floor
So I like him from a distance
My pen thanking him
for mere existence

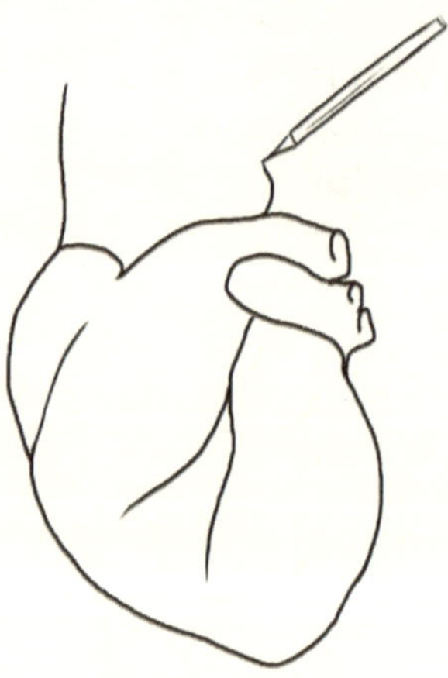

I touch your arm in the car
Fate leaves it there
and you don't complain

What do the fortune cards say?
They line the road in suites
Cups and Wands and Death
Although death is never what you expect
The future moves my hand to the wheel
so together we turn around
I let your gaze linger
With you I can't see her
Then I press all the buttons
on the dashboard
laughing as it changes nothing
You unbuckle your seatbelt
The end is the wild unknown
You want to become one with me
I pull the card with the skeleton
waiting to know what it means

Lead me to your bedroom
dreams are arbitrary
when there's you

Perhaps
we could learn to love
in quiet summer mornings
and bickering over groceries
We could hold hands
and become the people
we'll never really be
We could make lives
inside a bubble
not reality
We could
perhaps
maybe

I feel seen
when he remembers
what I have written
He drives to my house
for a lesson to be given
He's at my party
isn't that lovely
Assurances thrown in hedges
Promises and mountains
I can't believe the half of it
This attention
this wonderful friendship
This person willing
to surprise me
just to put a smile on me
It's more than I can put into words

The dark doesn't scare you
If you can't see them
then they can't see you

What if I can?

You're waiting at the traffic lights
waiting for my hand
We pull over
I drive for some time
You ask the dark
would this girl let herself be mine?

I turn off the engine but
colour floods my cheeks
It's only later in my bedroom
when I begin to think
I wonder if the other girl would mind?

You took me
in your arms
and carried me
to your bed

We kissed until
our clothes came off

but this was all
inside my head

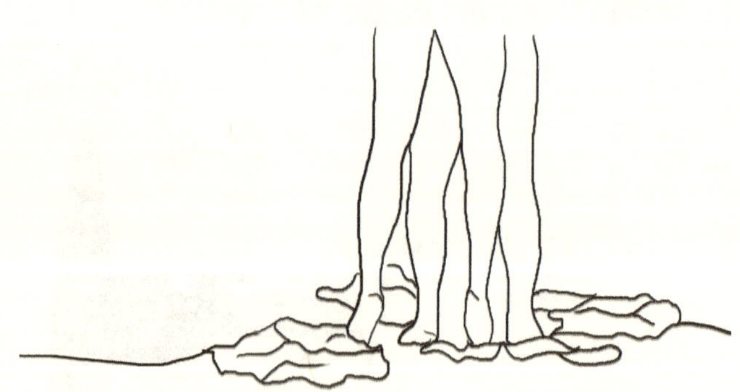

When the power goes out
I ask him to fix
more than just the electricity
inside my house
He cannot stomach
the thought of
losing my friendship
He likes to make
a positive difference
even at the cost of
my own convalescence
I repeat my former question
In answer he takes without hesitation
a puzzle piece of my fragility
with the intention to return it
after he makes it better
I start to call him my saviour
It feeds a certain muscle
I don't know what happened
to that missing piece of the puzzle

We can understand the rhythm
let it all go to our heads
It makes us buoyant
among the clouds
I let myself lose caution
I'm loud and you laugh
at the spectacle of it all
But a flash of concern
cuts me down to earth
I sway
Gravity has returned
She has a debt to pay
The poison lingers in my veins
I decide to use it anyway
Kiss me

You stop
Blink
Dawning
And gravity

Bathwater
the colour of twilight
He reads to me while
sitting against white tiles
Water droplets
cling to dark hair
I stir and the waves lap
a low moan of uncertainty
If I admit the unthinkable
that I believe I'm not beautiful
I wonder what he will do

I imagine him
nursing my spirit
until it blossoms

The real him
insists that I am beautiful
for I am sitting in her shadow

My room is perfumed with
midnight thoughts of you
The scent is strong
Daisies and vanilla and
the echo of something sinister
I unlatch a window
Fresh air only leaves me empty
The perfume is strangling
I've decided it's better than nothing

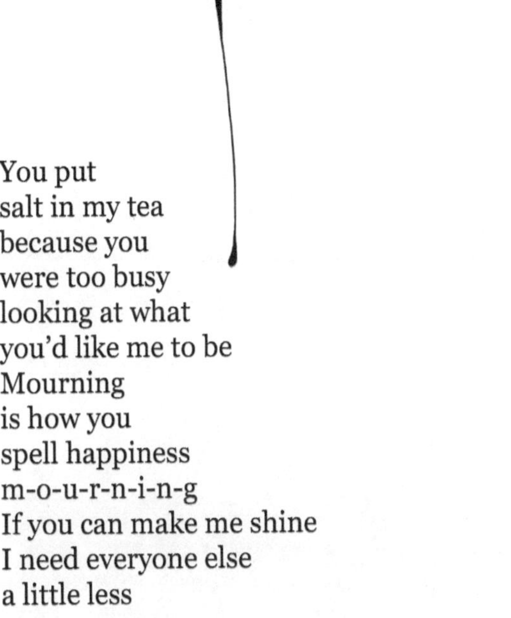

You put
salt in my tea
because you
were too busy
looking at what
you'd like me to be
Mourning
is how you
spell happiness
m-o-u-r-n-i-n-g
If you can make me shine
I need everyone else
a little less

You took me night driving
when I could no longer
feel the tears
although I knew they were there
still falling
never leaving

We lit joy in the headlights
found laughter under the dashboard
planted courage in the engine

I thought
you thought
we all thought
that it made us indispensable
A vehicle of good intention

He kissed my crown of hair
lingering as he said
I wish to hear each thought
that comes into your head
I heard his lips but not his eyes
What's the flavour of the lie
when what he says is sweet
but it's clouded in deceit
I'm not the only forehead
he kisses before sleep
I have trodden on fidelity
in the hope he might not leave
I watch the tail lights
fade away
My thoughts screaming
But I asked you to stay

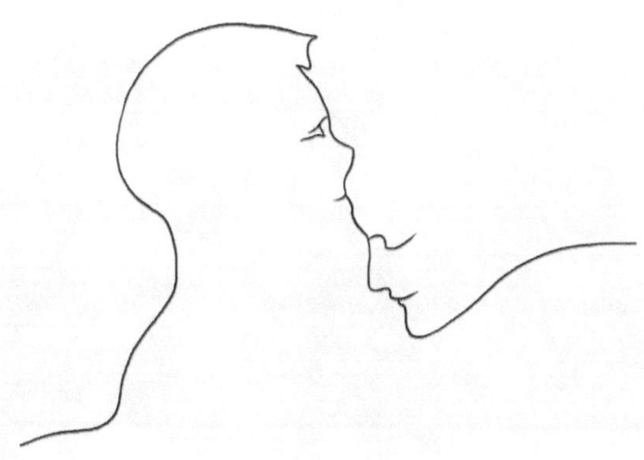

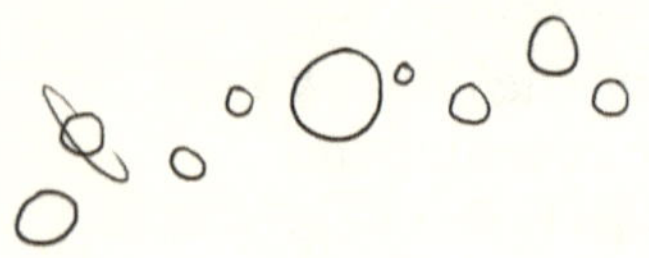

In mythology
you rule the planet
of unpredictable energy and
I fulfil the purpose of Mercury
carrying out requests
at the feet of the gods
adopting any personality
you are wanting to see

I saw him like no other
and mourned my empty bed
I wish he'd understood
and chosen me instead

He was my morning star
and my bright eclipse
My dawn
my dusk
my afternoon

The pulse
inside my wrist

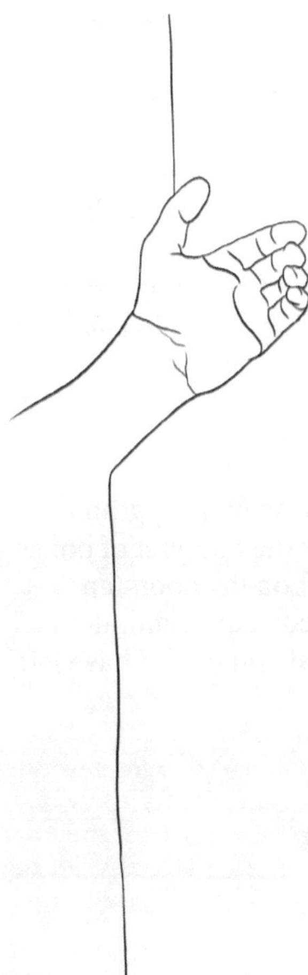

I'm caught inbetween
wanting to be free
and wanting you
to take care of me
You bury my body
so I can be with him
and I know it's wrong
beyond the grave are
watchful eyes
to disturb the dead is
a basic sin
in life we don't get
our indebted goodbyes

but I'm thanking you
as I swallow dirt and gravel
mouthful
after
mouthful

I'm so fucking grateful
for the bouquet of bones
left on my doorstep
A constant reminder
that you're all I have left

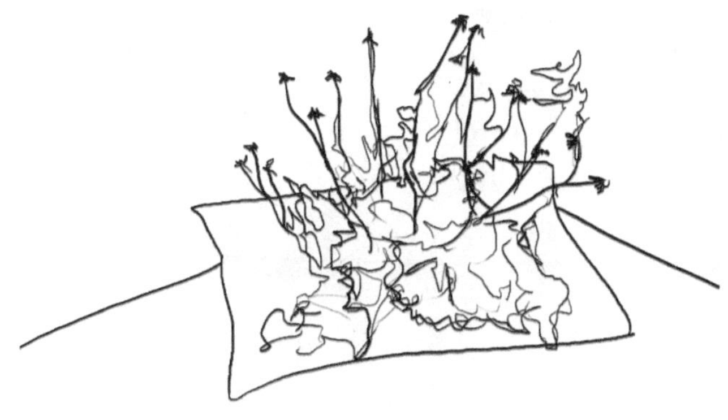

I go to bed with
your soft touch
and wake up next to
thistles and weeds

There's something
unnatural
growing inside me

Your hands played
with that soil
Water sprays my face
I trusted you with my garden

Did you plant
misery in your place?

I wrote us a story
Here's my pen
If you want you
can change the ending
or erase how it begins

Asked to undress
in sincerity and
Just trust me
I can save you
I only want
you to be happy

I spoke naked

A look
up and down

Dig deeper
was the command

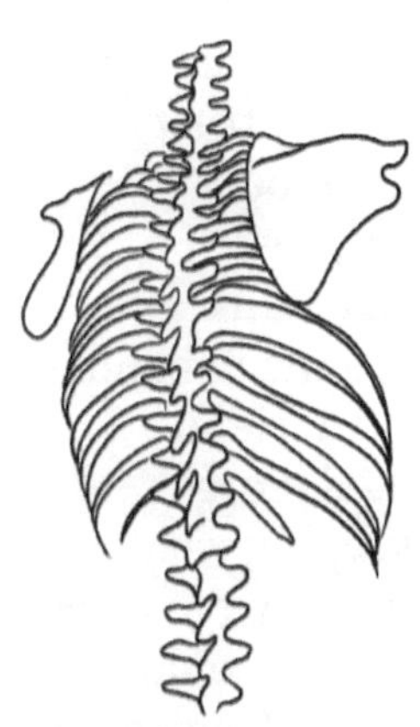

So I unhooked the
back of my head
and rolled my
flesh to the ground

I see right through you

The curl of a lip

Now let me play
with what you
have left

At the height of it was friendship
At the bottom
a kiss on the doorstep
A lie between my teeth
to keep the smile beneath
Betrayed my trust in
what could be
Took my grief
and made it his
strangled me in bandages
I wanted a friend
he wanted more
while keeping what was under him
I called to say I'm over it
He asks if he could stay a bit
I'm his ray of sunshine
blindfolding me
to what he'll always be
just another
disappointing line

The dolphin broke
the surface of the ocean
just so she could breathe
The echo of the seabed said
Is there nothing you have to say to me?

Men in fishing boats
advanced towards her
their nets woven in fury
Over one thousand
mutilated bodies
in rows upon the shore
The intelligent dolphins
breaking the ocean no more

She dived back under
to avoid the men
only to face the question again
Is there nothing you have to say to me?

The friendship is over
her heart told her
In the arms of the sea
she found relief

The next time she broke
the surface of the ocean
she was able to breathe alone

There are pins and needles
in my vascular organs
You give them a voice and
all my grief and insecurities
a foreboding importance

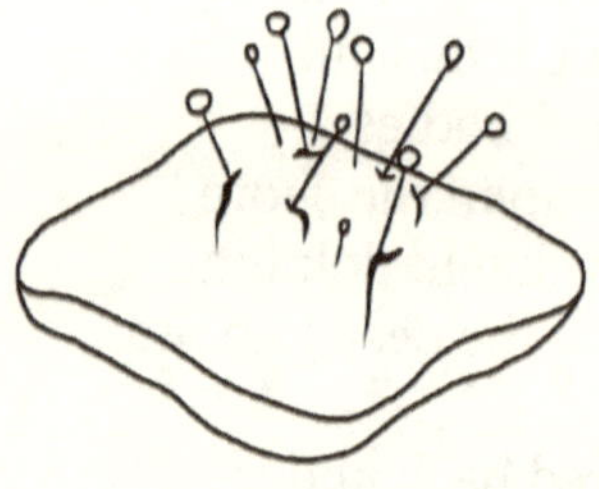

I came to you crawling
beaten and heart-bruised
You didn't blink or flinch
as I revealed the fractured
state of my ribs

I know now that you
were marvelling at
your own handiwork

You like to
dismantle the fragile
then put them
back together
the other way round

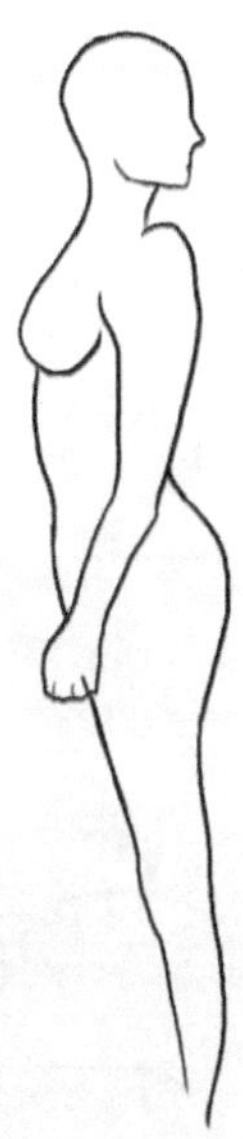

You pull words
from my mouth
tying the sentences
into something else
Are you trying to rewrite
what I'm made of?
Convince me that I'm every
crack in the ceiling
the tap that's always dripping
before you I am kneeling
while the overpass is screaming
and I am a language
without sense
Manipulated
under loving pretence

Cut me in two
it would be a miracle
to lose the half
I share with you

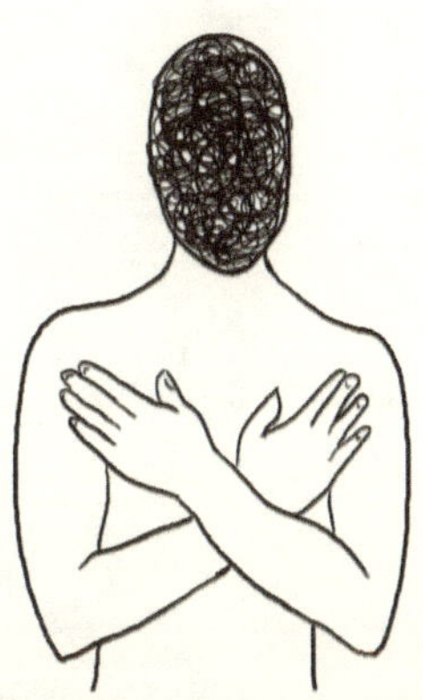

I gave you my feelings
and you kept them close
In the evening I felt beaten
Broken and unlovable
Selfish and expectant
The heaviest of all burdens
You digested them all
then tangled my emotions
in knotted explosions
and left me searching
for a way to untie them

The sky was a well of ink
bleak and starless
She wanted to dip her quill in
and watch the ripples
transcend to nothingness

I put myself on the line
and he cut the cord
So I toppled from the wire
my chest through his sword

There was a
stranger in
my bed last night
so I asked them
for their name
I blinked when
they turned over
I could have sworn
we were the same

He locked me
inside my own head
Silenced before
the draw of breath
He fears the shadow
of a third silhouette
The possibility that
it's him I might forget

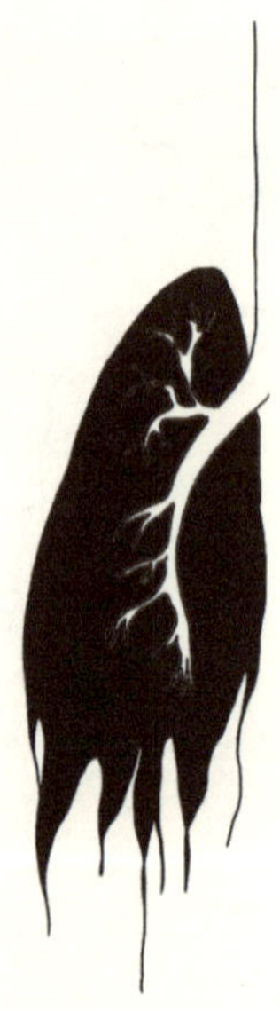

I wilt
and the ones who like to put
a conclusion on death
prosper
At least it was quick
At least it was painless
I blink
Painless?
All I am
is pain
and if the dead didn't suffer
then I am now suffering
for the both of us

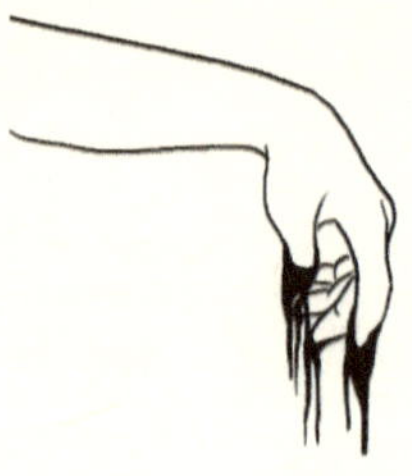

Is that potential on your fingertips?

I face my mirrors inwards
I cannot stand to see the picture
they insist on showing me
My reflection incases it all
I was looking for a saviour
and should have answered
my own call

Let's make a friendship
out of nothing but sand
There is the sea in the distance
I want to use it to help us stand

The one who wants to be my friend
longs to have me as something more
stares the water down
suspicion risen in every wave
No
they say
The sea is too unpredictable
You never know
when the tide will wash away

So we mould the friendship
on infidelity
twisting of realities
endless towers of pity

When the water eventually comes
the sandcastle is undone

I would like to apologise to the wife
To the girl at home
falling in love with the phone
remembering times when she didn't feel
as though she was just his stepping stone
The next time she calls
I will answer and tell her
That she is the microscopic mystery
hung up in the galaxy
too phenomenal for him to see
I am sorry
I am more sorry that
sorry is so overused
When I apologise
I hope she feels that whoosh of adrenaline
that fills your skin when you
kick off on a playground swing
I hope she remembers
the childlike anticipation of Christmas
the feeling of butterflies in her stomach
I hope sorry reminds her
that out there is adventure
she need only hang up the phone

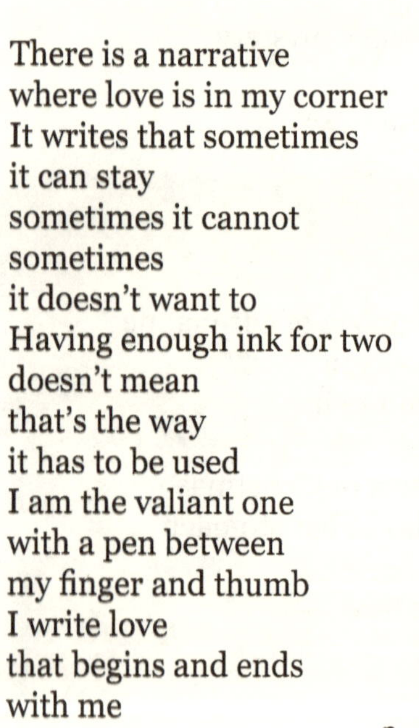

There is a narrative
where love is in my corner
It writes that sometimes
it can stay
sometimes it cannot
sometimes
it doesn't want to
Having enough ink for two
doesn't mean
that's the way
it has to be used
I am the valiant one
with a pen between
my finger and thumb
I write love
that begins and ends
with me

I bury my losses in my garden
ready to forget
I didn't anticipate them
growing into a tree
and demanding

Well what did you expect?

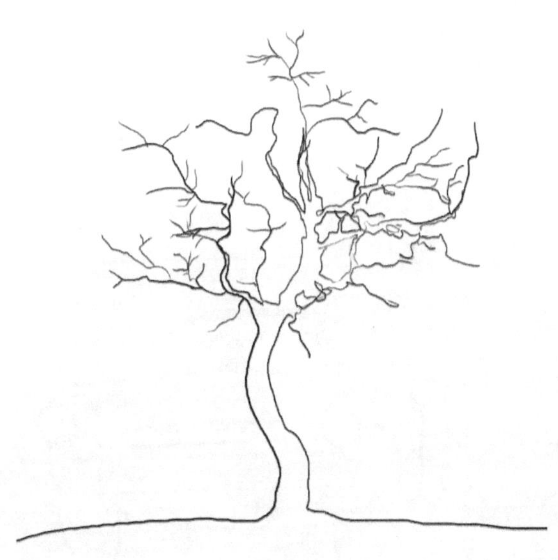

We're driving
through the exit sign
Pretty houses
suburban sights
It's nearly Halloween
when we eventually reach
the place we grew up
but won't grow old
You decide this is home

No

I point outward
There's a third silhouette

Home is there
over the bend
You just can't see it yet

My first kiss
was with myself
I hid inside my turtle shell
and kissed until my lips turned blue
I learnt to love
in my own two arms
I learnt how not to love
from you

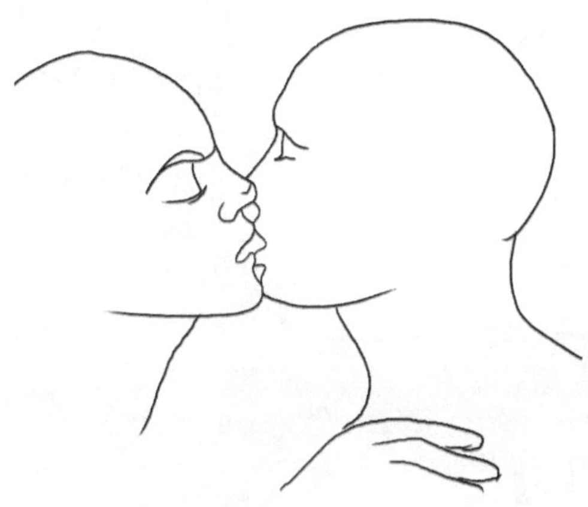

There's a gate at the end of the garden
just far enough out of reach
I tell everyone to put on their boots
and wear their warmest coats
We're going to walk through
anything to get there
I want to know what's
beyond the brick wall
what lies beneath
the evergreen hedge
if the iron gate will
open for all of us
or if I'm the only one
allowed ahead

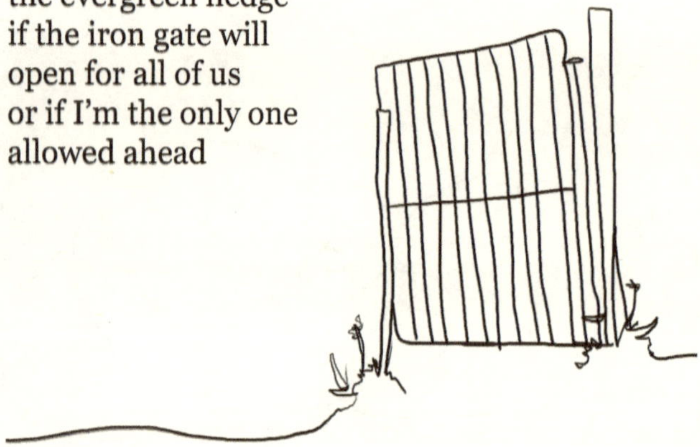

She let her hair down
her guard down
the people around
found issues with the length
the size of her independence
She believed
that the words she created
were empty houses
never homes
Until her best friend
called her past midnight
he said

My darling
When I read your piece
in the magazine
I heard the words
in the sound of your own voice
I had to call at this hour
I'm desperate to let you know
that it was in your writing
the paper just like concrete
where I finally found a home

Goodbyes
are inevitable
They crawl out
of hearts
and into necks
before getting
stuck in throats
Words have
nowhere to go
So looks are
passed
between us
A next time
we don't know

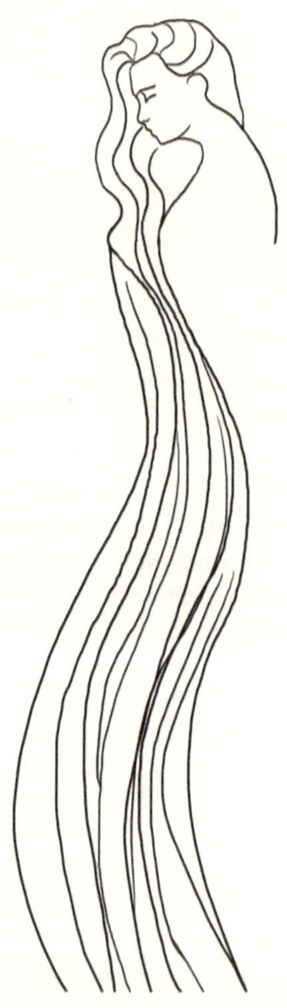

When his copy of the book arrives
he cracks open the spine
A year and a bit
since she apparently let slip
that her pen moved only in words
made for him
He runs a fever
oh-so-eager
to see himself in pages
drawn in love and hate
To his disappointment
he finds that all her poems
are not laced in his name
but in a confession
that she never wanted to be saved
She wanted a friend
who would listen and rub her shoulders
A friend who answered her calls
and most importantly
opened his own door
She wanted to meet
his girlfriend
go on car rides with all three of them
He cracks the spine further
trying to find his picture
when really
he isn't there at all

Where did we go in the night?
We got lost on Halloween
driving off an idea so obscene
The trees were tall and inviting
The stars in the sky enticing
But the moon sets
The sun rises
in consequence
A blindfold over my eyes
A song I sang to cover the lies
Where did we go in the night
that led to this demise

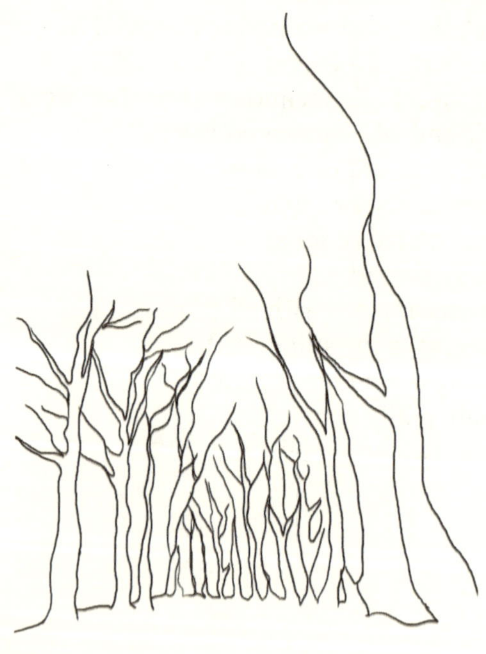

There is an email exchange at the finale
where the other end demands
Am I not worth the argument?
Hands hover over the keyboard
as I ponder a response
Honestly?
He was worth the argument
once
months ago
years ago
sometimes minutes ago
Then memory knocks on the door
hand-in-hand with sense
and I remember
that the argument
costs my energy
my budding sanctuary
those falling in love with me
I delete the email
I haven't heard from him since

Wasted potential
is what I'll call you
In time
I know I won't think of you
Only occassionally
like
on the bus next June
headphones on
trying to drown out the immediate crisis
with the currently playing song
Then the music skips
intentionally or my hand slips
It's the time you drove to my house
called me out
just to sit and sing
a ballad that was once a classic
I know all the lyrics
It's hilariously tragic
When the song ends
I leave the car
You say
Cute slippers
and drive away
I won't think of this again
until next June
when I'm sorry about what happened
but I don't want to reconcile with you

When my copy
of the book arrives
I smile
For it's the first time
in a long time
that I feel completely
myself

It rained on the first day of mourning
It rained when I felt tomorrow coming
My cousin calls it pathetic fallacy
My English teacher would agree
I may have lost a father
but I still have a sister and a mother
It rains when I miss them
when I cry for those lost years

Tears and water and grieving
make the ground sound enough
for growing
There is a life in me

I bathe daily in saltwater

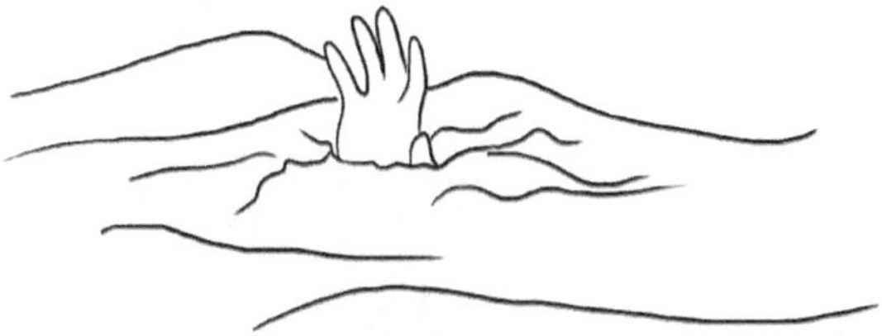

Reclaim the memories
I know they're hard to hear
You have to make
them your own again
There's more to come
that you'll hold dear

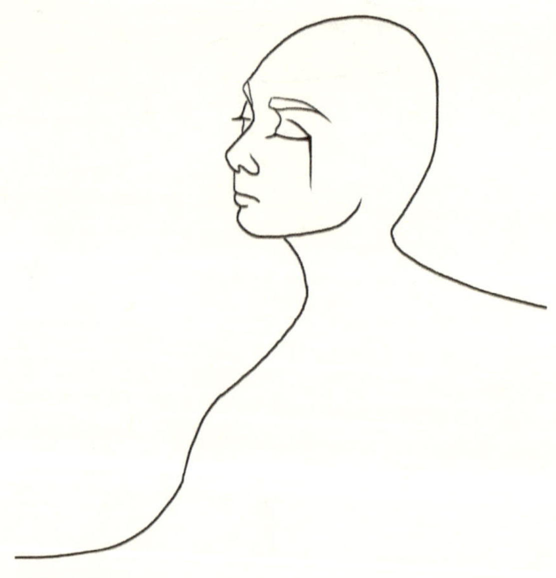

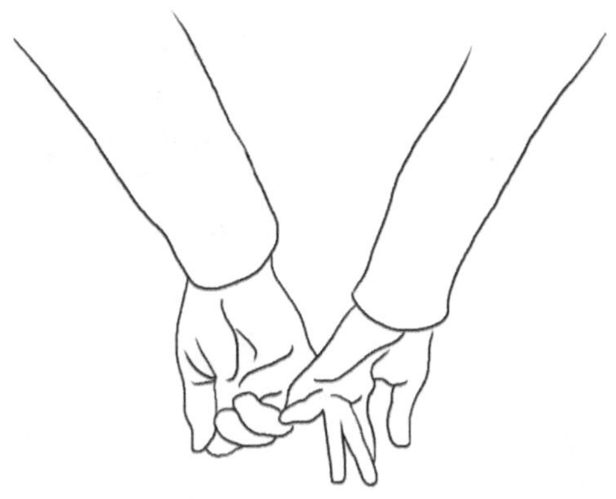

That's not my hand
I say
The moon smiles
Really?
I inspect it closer
That's not my hand
I insist
Really?
Because I think it's
your hand
and not his

There's a pricking
Life is wicked
I have you
and someone
else coming

He will
dance with me in the kitchen
and cook risotto for tea
The weather isn't a bother
although he prefers the summer
he just wants to hold hands with me
He will
introduce me
to my old self
Encourage me to reconcile
My brain and body finally have a talk
agree to disagree until they agree
to love the other for what they are
and not what they could be
He will
throw seeds like confetti
It's a celebration to change
He will be a human
with problems
and annoyances
There will be disagreements
Grief
however
will never be the core of it
He will be the first face
in the morning
The name upon my lips

My father would have loved you
adored the conversation
spreading words into hours
the way he liked to spread
butter on bread
My father would have loved you
counting and listening
supporting what you do
He would have loved
how you love me
He would have seen
what I still see
He would have—

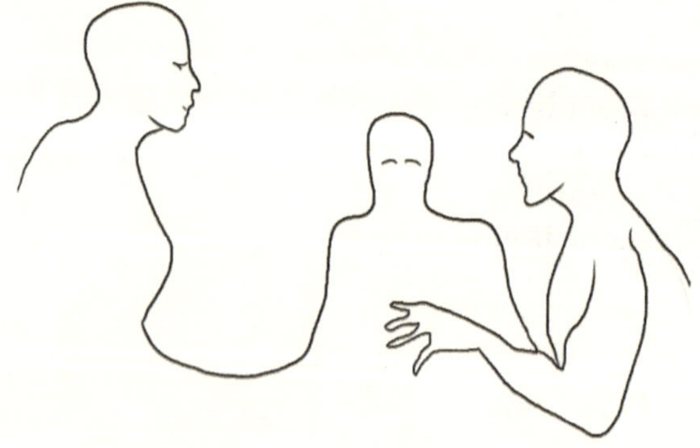

The cure is in the hemisphere
The way the night-time breaks
For you it's dark and icy
today my sun will wake
It rises in the form of
two little fingers
brushing each other
wanting to lock in a promise
We'll be friends and lovers
and everything for forever
or until forever is over
whichever one comes first
Hands to help the other stand
not to hammer nails through
I'm finding my own saving
being in tandem with you

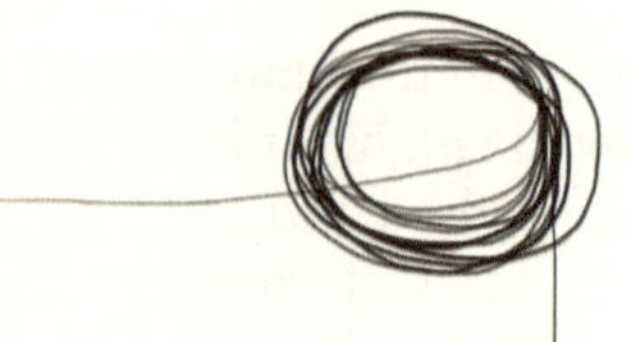

He is the full moon
bleeding through my blinds
the colours that aren't in the sunrise
He is swimming in the ocean after dark
the call in the forest of a distant lark
He's the gentle sun beating on my skin
the taste of butter and sweet cinnamon
He's the lowest note in a jazz song
He's where I wanted to be all along

Looks fade and beauty
vanishes like dust on a desert
There is someone who makes
the core of your belly ache
who encourages laughter
holds you in honesty
dreams of you in waking
Love them in return

My dad had a record collection
stacked up in his study
Mostly symphonies
but he squeezed Mozart and Beethoven
between Queen
We watched a documentary
on Freddie Mercury one summer
I had come home with a pink face
from too much sun
to sit on the couch upstairs with him
eating chocolate spread on toast
After the program finished
he went into his study and came back
with a faded white record sleeve
We listened to the first track and the second
Then the third
We listened until the music stopped
but the record kept spinning
Life ends and the world keeps moving
silent and with ears straining
to remember the sound of those gone
My father left an imprint on me
I remember him in music
Classical
Jazz
and Queen
I feel him still with me
the way it's always been

Have you ever seen a dead body?

I'm on my side
his nose pressed to mine
There are last words
unknown
The sun is open
No one's home
I stopped having the dreams
The ones where my father
would visit me
Did I let go or did he?
I hope you never have to see a dead body
But if you do
I'll stroke your hair
kiss your cheek
guide you through the recovery

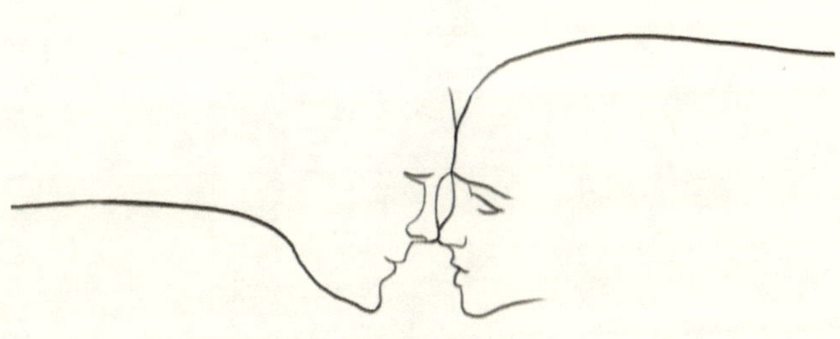

I imagine running in to her
at the supermarket
She asks if I'm the same
rose her boyfriend grew
from a seed
I tell her it only appeared that way
it's easy to hide scissors in
intentions called love
Our small talk dribbles on
I see the end nearing
my heart reaches out

He's a chameleon
He changes
according to what he
thinks you should see

In her eyes there is dawning
then
gravity

I take down the wallpaper
Paint the space over
with friends who encourage laughter
sisters who show me how to pick lavender
the smell of my grandmother's cooking
boys who find assertiveness good looking
I make a home in those
who answer after midnight
who find me after a fight
take the time
not to ask
to make sure
that I'm all right
I frame a piece of old wallpaper
Hang it by the door
Every time when I walk in
I'm reminded
of where I am
against a portrait
of where I've been

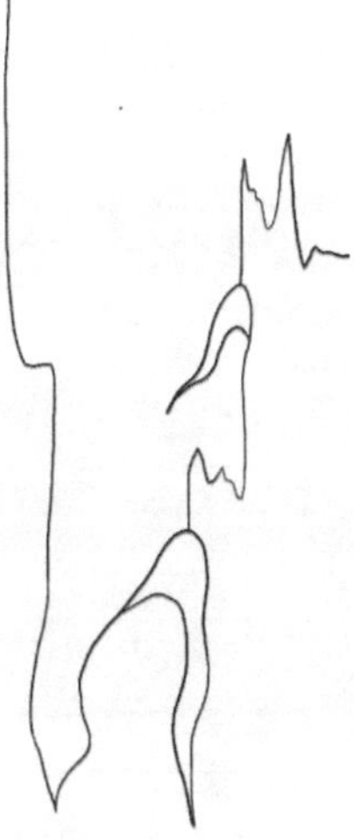

He liked picking me up
and dropping me off places
even though he was as punctual
as I am not
I still don't really know how
to abide by the clock
He liked it all the same
Late nights
After school
After choir
Before school
A friend's house
The beach
I don't know why
Most kids took the bus
But dad honestly liked picking me up
He said it's what fathers did
He was wrong
Only some fathers were like that
And he was the best of all

From grief
beautiful things
are born

My cousin eyes me
offers a cigarette
I give her a look
She shrugs
Now is as good a time as any
My sister messages me from the airport
She's running late for her flight
We both feel Dad rolling his eyes
I bled for healing arms
and drained out in the process
Forgot about my family
my mother holding a tourniquet
I'm strong but still so delicate
They're the only ones with
a slip of understanding
They leave a trail of breadcrumbs
whenever I feel like returning

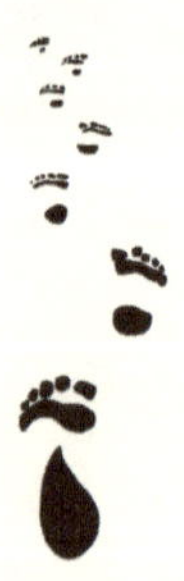

abbie amy

The trees in transition
from autumn to winter
They lose the part of themselves
not needed for the coming season
A forest adapts to the will
of the world
I want to emulate nature

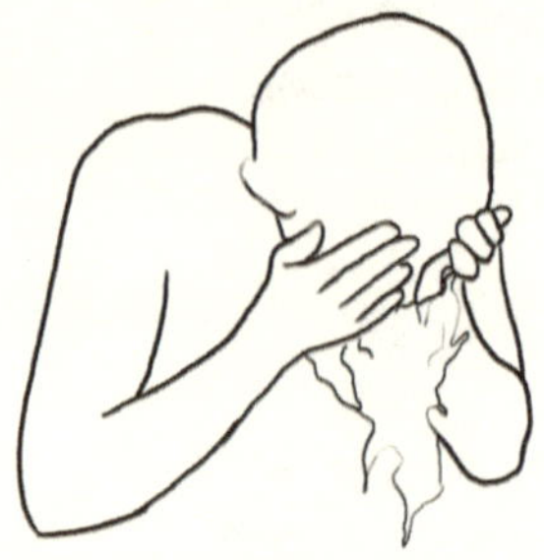

It's the sigh of the soul
punctured to let out
the trapped resentment
It's the slow heat of the day
a washed face in the morning
the turn of the page
I'll be able to write
something new
after knowing you

and I do

I do
I do
I do

I am seated at the piano
Hands you already know
Leaving fingerprints
on sheets of music
you can turn to when I go
You like the way my hair flicks up
and how I dust myself in sugar
I play the song you started
when I stood with you last Christmas
There's an octave undiscovered
the final note to come

I will see the old
with new eyes
cut from perspective
I will not regret because
I cannot change what
has already happened
I will turn around to
meet my reflection
the one on the inside
the one who cannot lie
She tells me it's time
to join her outside

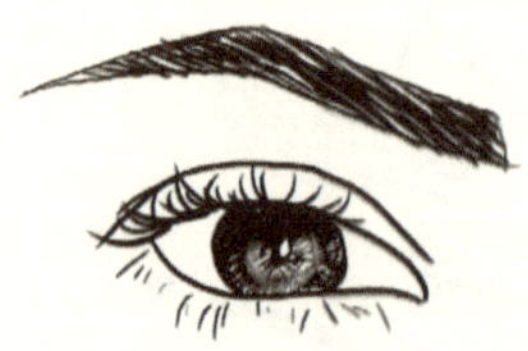

There's a girl walking across the street
Katniss braid and leggings
smiling at her phone screen
She is and isn't me

Hang up with I love you
I want to tell her
Be kinder to your father
Don't underestimate your mother
You'll be in and out of life
In and out of boundaries
In and out
Success comes in waves
You'll be sad and happy on the same day
and at eighteen
you'll know what it is to be brave
Your hero is Katniss Everdeen
it's going to take six years to understand
what that actually means

There's a girl across the street
who is and isn't me
I wish I could give her these words
show her how far she's going to travel
when it feels like she's standing still

That girl is walking her way across years
making her way to me

Sometimes in the silence
I hear all the voices
of my past life shouting
to me in unison

We are so proud of you

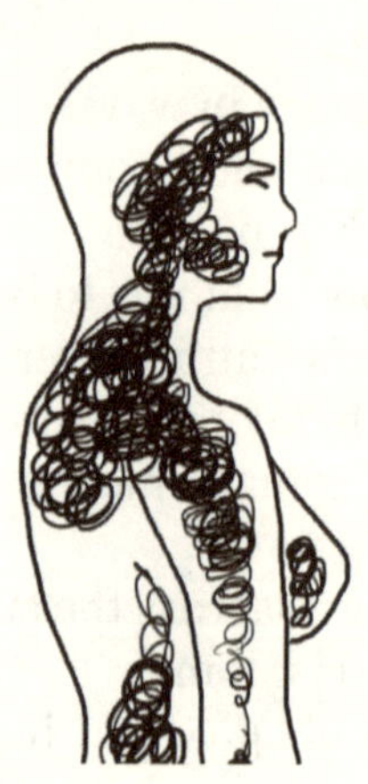

When love comes to bed
I put my head against his chest
It's a day in July
too hot for sleeping
I tell his body
about a birthday
we should be celebrating
Cake and unlit candles and
balloons without any helium
Love gets me tissues and water
and buckets of care
He reminds me that
birthdays are still important
even when life can't be there
This love
I can see it in his eyes
he longs to do it for me
But this love knows
that it has to come
from my own story
He says we'll light
the candles tomorrow
the birthday wishes will keep
I reach out to love
and thank him
Together we fall asleep

—Dad's Birthday

I was so focused
on the night
that I neglected
the importance of day

I laugh
in the face
of adversary
The challenges
regard me with caution
their pupils
dilated and wary
I am laughing everyday
Life doesn't pause
once you've been bruised
It kicks and takes before
the monster wakes
and I laugh
because I remember
that compared to others
I have it better
I laugh until
my cheeks ache
I will laugh through
each and every heartbreak

Let yourself
settle your roots
if this is the garden
that you choose
Nurture your nature
Plant your woe
There's someone
who will love you better
She's the girl you already know

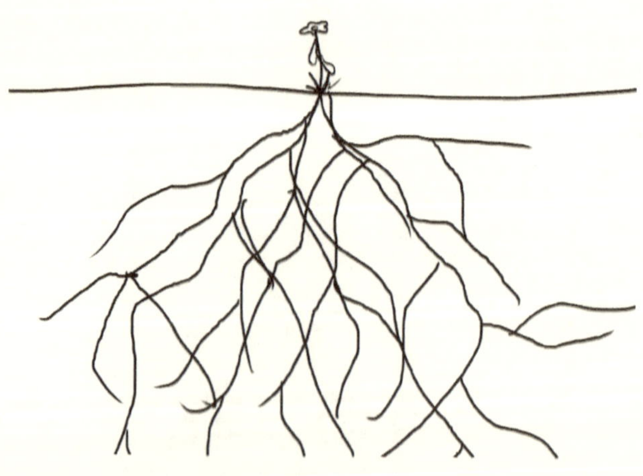

Getting up early
Breathing in
the morning
Brewing tea
Wondering in a year
just who I will be
There is change in the
hot water
stir in the sugar
Waking up before
the sun does
just so I can
burn brighter

You have come to the end
Unfortunately I haven't
for grief never truly ends
You will close this
stop listening
go on with your living
And I want you to
I also want you to know
that I will always bleed
Why should I live with loss quietly?
It has taken me five years
to graduate with this knowledge
It's a Ferris wheel
swinging me from high to low
Sometimes the beautiful times
are terrifying times
for you anticipate the drop
What goes up must come down but
they don't tell you
that it always comes back around
Perhaps you're like me
You survive with the dead too
If you are then remember
that you are filled with wonder
no person is a shield
This isn't for them
This was only ever for you

And there is nothing
but shapes and water
A decision to breathe
before you reach after

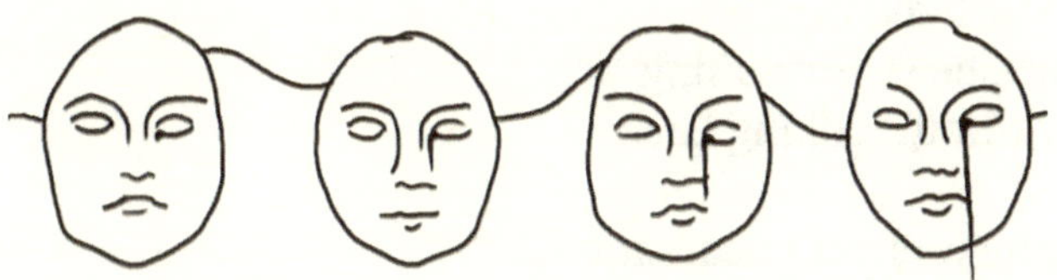

She said
It isn't over
every tiny atom
awoke inside her
The moon smiled
and pointed out
much like a mirror

*The dreams that
don't come true
make way for
the ones that do*

She liked that
so she set off sailing
without looking back

She was out of earshot
when the moon spoke again

*There's someone waiting
for you there*

just over the bend

To

Mum, Dad and Katie

Sidney Jean
Andrew Fraser
Florence Wood
Lena Krakowian
Miriam Briggs
Nafisha Nulwala
Emily Corris
Allegra Williams

and Georgie Carpenter.

Thank you. For love. For kindness.

For letting me write.

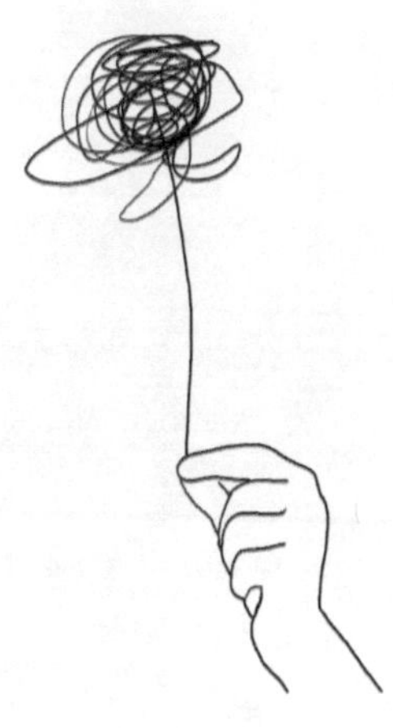

The Writer

Abbie Amy is a self-confessed love poet, writer and artist. She lives in London, writing about friendships, family and the people she sees on the tube.

You can find her writing online at www.abbieamy.com and on Instagram @booksbyabbie.

Ink for Two is her first collection of poetry.

The Artist

Sidney Jean is a Melbourne-based artist, designer and editor studying Professional Writing and Editing at RMIT University. As well as illustrating Ink for Two, she writes short stories and nonfiction in her own time.

You can find her work on Instagram @sidney_jean.